World Book's Learning Ladders

Animal Homes

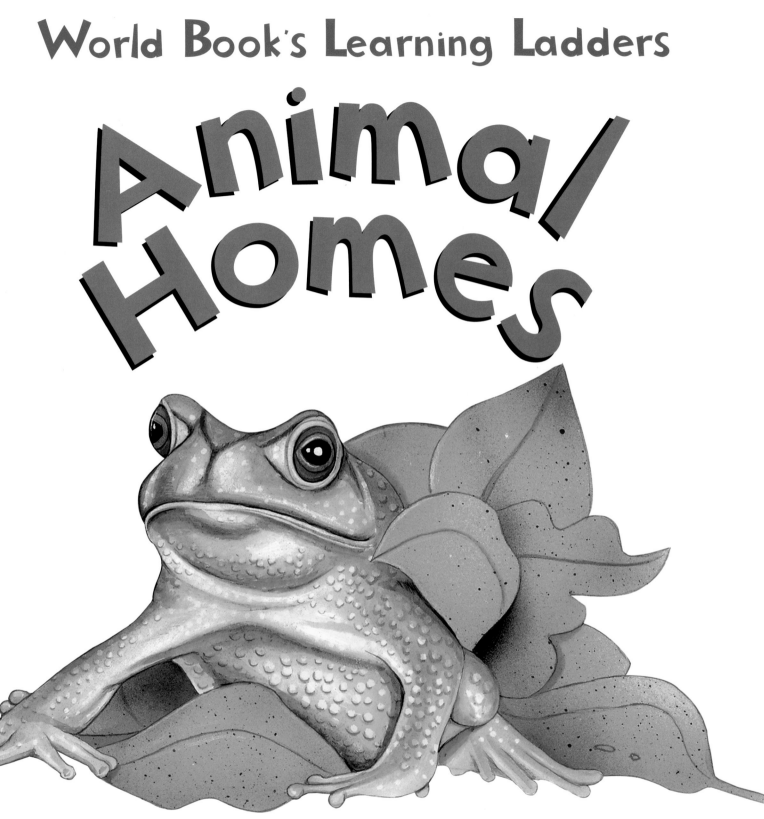

WORLD
BOOK

a Scott Fetzer company
Chicago

www.worldbookonline.com

WORLD BOOK

233 N. Michigan Avenue
Chicago, IL 60601
U.S.A.

For information about other World Book publications, visit our website at
http://www.worldbook.com or call **1-800-WORLDBK (967-5325).**

For information about sales to schools and libraries, call **1-800-975-3250 (United States);**
1-800-837-5365 (Canada).

2008 revised printing

Library of Congress Cataloging-in-Publication Data

Animal homes.
    p. cm. -- (World Book's learning ladders)
  Summary: "Introduction to animal homes using
simple text, question and answer format, illustrations,
and photos. Features include puzzles and games, fun
facts, a resource list, and an index"--Provided by
publisher.
  Includes bibliographical references and index.
  ISBN 978-0-7166-7726-0
  1. Animals--Habitations--Juvenile literature.
I. World Book, Inc.
QL756.A536 2007
591.56'4--dc22
              2007018907

World Book's Learning Ladders
Set ISBN: 978-0-7166-7725-3

Printed in China by Shenzhen Wing King Tong Paper
Products Co., Ltd.
Shenzhen, Guangdong
7th printing May 2013

Editor in Chief: Paul A. Kobasa

Supplementary Publications
  Associate Director: Scott Thomas
  Managing Editor: Barbara A. Mayes

Senior Editor: Shawn Brennan

Editor: Dawn Krajcik

Researcher: Cheryl Graham

Manager, Contracts & Compliance
  (Rights & Permissions): Loranne K. Shields

Graphics and Design
  Associate Director: Sandra M. Dyrlund
  Associate Manager, Design: Brenda B. Tropinski
  Associate Manager, Photography: Tom Evans

Production
  Director, Manufacturing and Pre-Press: Carma Fazio
  Manager, Manufacturing: Steven Hueppchen
  Production Technology Manager: Anne Fritzinger
  Proofreader: Emilie Schrage

This edition is an adaptation of the Ladders series
published originally by T&N Children's Publishing, Inc.,
of Minnetonka, Minnesota.

Photographic credits: Cover: © Artur Tabor, Nature Picture Library; p4: Planet Earth Pictures;
p6: Planet Earth Pictures; p7: Papilio Photographic; p9: William Osborn/BBC Natural History
Unit; p11: Oxford Scientific Films; p15: Planet Earth Pictures; p16: Bruce Coleman Ltd;
p18: Power Stock/Zefa; p20: Tony Stone Images; p21: David Fleetham/Oxford Scientific Films;
p22: Kit Houghton Photography; p23: © Andrew Linscott, Alamy Images.

Illustrators: Fiametta Dogi, James Evans, John Butler

What's inside?

This book tells you about lots of different animal homes. You can find out where animals live—from high up in the treetops to deep underground—and how they build their amazing homes.

Holes and tunnels

Deep under the ground in the dark, moles, rabbits, and badgers live in long tunnels and snug holes. The big picture shows a mole hard at work, digging and scooping up earth to make its new underground home.

A **mole** usually lives alone. It spends most of its time in the dark.

A European rabbit's underground home is called a warren. When the coast is clear, the rabbit hops out and nibbles the grass.

A mole's underground tunnel is called a **burrow**. Inside, there are tasty worms for the mole to eat.

Strong **paws** shaped like shovels are perfect for moving earth.

It's a fact!

A badger is a busy housekeeper! On a warm day, the badger drags its bedding outside the burrow to air it in the sun.

A mound of earth piles up above the ground. This is called a **molehill**.

The mole kicks away earth with its **back legs**.

Baby moles sleep in a cozy room called a **chamber**.

5

Dens

Many animals make secret, hideaway homes in rocky caves and hollow tree trunks. These homes are called dens. In the big picture, a grizzly bear and its young are inside their warm cave.

A pile of **branches** keeps the cave hidden and warm.

In winter, this bear stays in its **cave**.

A young fox peeks out of its den in a tree trunk. In springtime, it's warm enough to come out and play!

The **rocky walls** of a cave keep out snow and wind.

Huge groups of bats live in caves. They sleep here all day long, hanging upside down. It's a tight squeeze!

A pile of leaves makes a soft **bed**.

A sleepy baby bear, called a **cub**, snuggles up to its mother.

7

Treehouses

It's safe high up in the trees! Hungry enemies are far below on the ground. Squirrels build nests, while a noisy woodpecker drills a hole into a thick tree trunk.

It's a fact!

A tent bat camps out in the trees! The bat folds a leaf into a tent shape, then hides underneath.

A squirrel's **bushy tail** helps it keep its balance in the treetops.

These squirrels are building their round **nest** on a strong branch.

8

Soft **moss** keeps the inside of the nest warm and cozy.

Woven **twigs** and grass make the nest firm and strong.

A woodpecker taps at a tree with its long, sharp beak for hours. It makes a round hole, where it will live.

9

Logs and leaves

All kinds of tiny creatures make their homes on a mossy log. Here, they can sleep, eat, hunt, and lay their eggs. When the log becomes too crowded, the pile of leaves next door makes a safe place to shelter, too!

A shiny beetle crawls over the **moss**, looking for a crack where it can lay its eggs.

A beetle's eggs hatch into wriggling grubs that chew **wood** for their dinner.

Millipedes curl up under the **bark** where it is damp and dark.

A spider finds plenty to eat on the log. It spins a **web** to catch a juicy insect.

Weaver ants glue leaves together to make a nest. The queen ant, the most important ant of all, lays her eggs here.

This toad is cool and safe under a mound of fallen, decaying **leaves**.

A centipede is a fierce hunter. It chases spiders and beetles across the **log**.

In the woods

The woods are full of animal homes! Take a look high up in the trees, under piles of leaves, and near old, mossy logs.

12

How does the noisy woodpecker drill a hole in the tree?

What is the squirrel carrying to help build its home?

Words you know

Here are some words that you read earlier in this book. Say them out loud, then try to find the things in the picture.

molehill   den
bark   moss
twigs   web

How many bumpy molehills are popping out of the ground?

Birds' nests

In spring, many birds build comfortable nests, where they lay eggs. Soon the eggs hatch into hungry, noisy baby birds. The nest is home to the baby birds until they grow strong enough to look after themselves.

It's a fact!

Friendly birds called weavers live in apartments! Together, they build a big, grassy nest with a doorway for each bird.

A mother duck builds her **nest** near the edge of a lake.

She sits on her **eggs** to keep them warm.

Soft, fluffy **feathers** line the nest.

A stork builds a huge nest that it returns to every year. This stork's nest is perched on top of a tall chimney!

A baby duck is called a **duckling**.

Tall **reeds** and cattails grow around the nest.

Hives and insect nests

A wasp nest is home to hundreds of striped wasps. Honey bees live together too, in homes called hives. Inside the hives, the bees make sweet honey that is delicious to eat.

Every week, a beekeeper visits the hive. He wears a mask and gloves to protect himself from the bees' sharp stings.

The queen wasp lays lots of tiny white **eggs**.

Each egg has its own special room, called a **cell**.

This **wasps' nest** hangs down from the branch of a tree.

It's a fact!

A honey bee fills cells with honey. When a cell is full, the bee makes a lid and covers the cell— just like putting a lid on a jar.

The eggs hatch into fat **grubs** that eat all day long!

Worker wasps chew wood to make **paper** to build the nest.

Lodges

A family of hard-working beavers help each other to build a home on the river. They use branches, sticks, and thick, brown mud. The big picture shows you what their home looks like above and below the water.

A beaver carries a **branch** in its mouth.

The family home is called a **lodge**. It makes a dam across the river.

A beaver gnaws at a tree with its strong front teeth. Before long, the whole tree will fall over. *Crash!*

Sticky brown **mud** holds the branches firmly together.

Baby beavers stay snug and dry in a room above the water.

Beavers swim in and out of the lodge through a **tunnel**.

Shells

A few animals carry their homes around with them, wherever they go! A slimy snail has a shell on its back. In dry weather, the snail hides inside the shell, but when it's wet, it pokes out its head in search of tasty food.

A **snail** crawls along, searching for juicy leaves to munch.

A tortoise lives inside its tough shell. When the tortoise goes to sleep, it pulls its head into its shell.

Feelers help the snail to find its way around.

A hard, round **shell** covers the snail's soft body. The shell is the snail's home.

A hungry **bird** is on ....
the lookout for a
tasty snail to eat.

When a snail is
frightened, it pulls
its **head** into its shell.

.... As a snail crawls
along, it leaves a
shiny, gooey **trail**.

A hermit crab doesn't have its own shell,
so it borrows one! When the crab grows
too big for the shell, it finds a new one.

Pets' homes

It can be great fun looking after a pet. There are lots of different kinds to choose from. Wild animals take care of themselves, but pets need people to give them food, water, and a clean, safe home.

Goldfish dart around and nibble on plants in a **tank** of fresh water.

A horse rests in a stable, but it also enjoys being outside in a field, where it can gallop and eat grass.

A hamster's home is like a playground with an **exercise wheel** and more!

A parakeet flies out of its **cage** to exercise.

A soft bed is an excellent place for a dog to sleep and hide toys and bones!

In warm weather, guinea pigs scamper in an outdoor **pen**.

By the river

Many animals live by the river—in the trees, on the grassy banks, and even in the water itself.

Can you find the pet animals in the field?

24

Words you know

Here are some words that you read earlier in this book. Say them out loud, then try to find the things in the picture.

ducklings   wasps' nest

shells   branch

field   lodge

Where has the mother duck made her cozy nest?

25

Did you know?

Wild beavers often play tricks on each other!

To avoid bumping into each other, moles tap their heads against the sides of their tunnels. This sends vibrations through the earth and warns other moles to stay away!

A woodpecker's nest may extend 6 to 18 inches (15 to 45 centimeters) below the entrance.

Most cave bats spend each winter in the same place and each summer in the same roost.

During hot, dry spells, toads dig deep into the ground and remain there.

A squirrel usually has more than one nest and can move quickly to another nest if threatened.

Puzzles

Close-up!

We've zoomed in on three different animal homes. Can you figure out which homes they are?

1

2

3

Answers on page 32.

Link the pairs!

Can you link the pairs of animals that live in the same kind of home? The questions below will help you.

rabbit

snail

bat

tortoise

bear

mole

Which two animals...

1 ...live in a burrow underground?

2 ...live inside a shell that they carry on their back?

3 ...might you find in a cozy cave?

Match up!

Match each word on the left with its picture on the right.

1. nest

2. hive

3. lodge

4. tank

5. den

6. pen

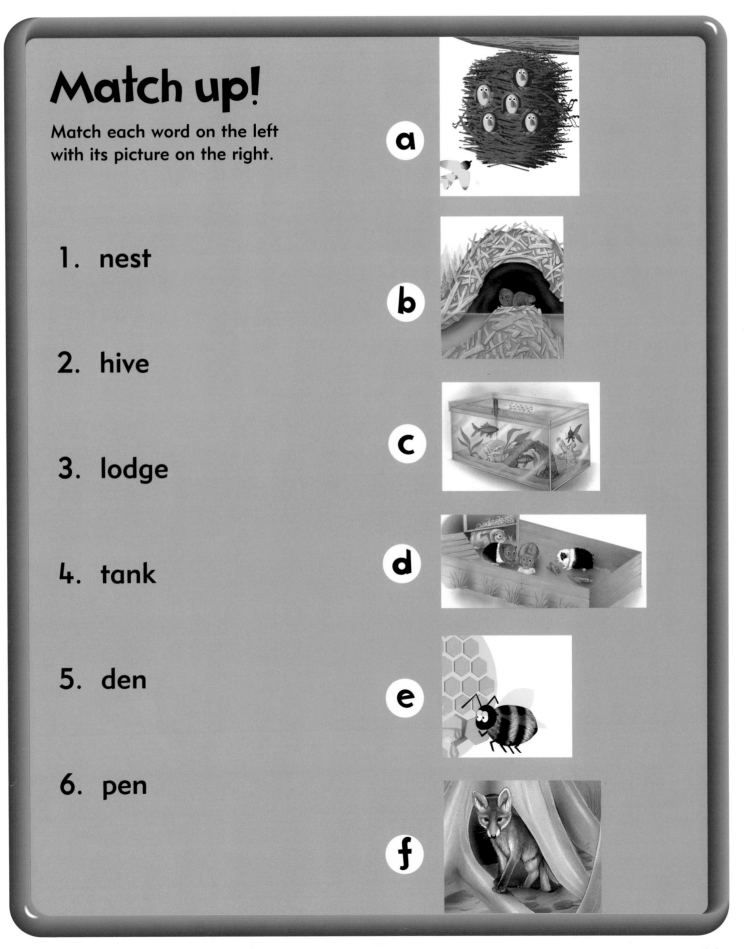

Answers on page 32.

True or false

Can you figure out which of these statements are true? Turn to the page numbers given to help you find the answers.

3 A badger drags its bedding outside to air it in the sun.
Go to page 5.

1 A weaver lives in a hole in the ground.
Go to page 14.

4 A honey bee seals a honey cell with a lid.
Go to page 17.

2 A tent bat lives in a snug tent made out of a leaf.
Go to page 8.

5 A beaver nearly always knows which way a tree will fall.
Go to page 19.

Answers on page 32.

Find out more

Books

Animals at Work: How Animals Build, Dig, Fish and Trap, Etta Kaner (Kids Can Press, 2001)
Animals use some surprising skills to build structures for themselves, and this book tells how they do it.

Animals Don't Wear Pajamas: A Book About Sleeping, Eve B. Feldman (Henry Holt, 1992)
Where do animals go when they sleep? Find out what 16 animals use for their beds.

Homes, Victoria Parker (Heinemann Library, 2006)
Find out why animals need shelter as much as people do, and how they go about getting it.

Peaceful Moments in the Wild: Animals and Their Homes, Stephanie Maze (Moonstone Press, 2002)
Photographs of 13 animals in their homes show the many different kinds of places around the world where our wild friends live.

Strange Nests, Ann Shepard Stevens (Millbrook Press, 1998)
This book looks at the nests of 11 different kinds of birds, from the tiny hummingbird to the huge eagle.

Web sites

Animal Homes, Kidport Reference Library
http://www.kidport.com/RefLib/Science/AnimalHomes/AnimalHomes.htm
This Web site groups animal homes into nine different types, such as rock caves, tree homes, and water homes. Click on a group for descriptions and photos of the animals who live there.

Animal Homes, North Mississippi Grades K-8 Project
http://smartweed.olemiss.edu/nmgk12/curriculum/elementary/third/Animal%20Homes%20Project%2073.doc
Read about the different kinds of animal homes, then test your knowledge with a quiz.

Animal Homes, Pub Quiz Help
http://www.pubquizhelp.34sp.com/animals/homes.html
An alphabetical list of 28 animals pairs with another list of the names of their homes: for example, cat to cattery, fox to den, and snake to nest.

Feather Their Nests, FamilyFun.com
http://familyfun.go.com/decorating-ideas/gardening/feature/famf0804birds/famf0804birds.html
This family activity gives you a chance to help birds build their nests.

Houses, Dragonfly Web Pages
http://www.units.muohio.edu/dragonfly/houses
See what it's like to be a hermit crab or a bat and live in your very special home.

Answers

Puzzles
from pages 28 and 29

Close-up!
1. wasps' nest
2. snail's shell
3. beavers' lodge

Link the pairs!
1. rabbit and mole
2. snail and tortoise
3. bat and bear

Match up!
1. a
2. e
3. b
4. c
5. f
6. d

True or false
from page 30

1. false
2. true
3. true
4. true
5. true

Index